6

Public Policies Should Help the Elderly Live at Home

National Association of Area Agencies on Aging

The National Association of Area Agencies on Aging (N4A) is the umbrella organization for the 655 area agencies on aging in the United States. N4A's primary mission is to help older people and those with disabilities live with dignity in their homes and communities for as long as possible.

Aging adults overwhelmingly want to remain in their own homes as opposed to living in a nursing home or board and care center. In a 1999 ruling known as the *Olmstead* decision, the U.S. Supreme Court agreed that elderly and disabled people should be able to live in the community in the least restrictive setting possible. However, even though home care is better for seniors and cheaper than nursing homes, current public policies still favor institutionalization of the elderly. National public policies should be changed to support home care and community-based services in order to best address the medical, social, and environmental needs of the old.

As individuals age, and chronic conditions increase, the need for long-term care services grows. Long-term care refers to a broad range of services, paid and unpaid and provided in a variety of settings, for persons who need assistance with daily activities due to a physical or mental limitation. The availability of formal or informal support and services, an individual's needs and preferences and the ability to finance needed services all play a part in determining the setting in which an individual will receive long-term care services. According to a recent General Accounting Office (GAO) report, of the almost six million adults age 65 and over with long-term care needs, only 20 percent receive care services in a nursing home or other institutional setting, with the remaining 80 percent receiving assistance at home and in the community. Home and community-based care, which allows individuals to maintain their independence and age with dignity in the comfort of their own homes, in familiar neighborhoods and communities, is overwhelmingly the preferred choice of older adults, as well as individuals with disabilities.

Our federal policies do not adequately recognize that the most cost-effective form of long-term care is provided through home and community-based services. These services are currently provided through a fragmented and inconsistent array of federal, state, local, and private support services paid for through public and private financing. Moreover, despite the substantial role that family caregivers play in providing long-term care, the United States lacks a coherent set of policies to assist informal caregivers. Demographic changes, the aging of the 77 million baby-boomers, and increasing longevity will intensify current delivery and financing difficulties.

Olmstead Decision Calls for Least Restrictive Setting

The 1999 Supreme Court *Olmstead v. L.C.* decision has accelerated the shift of national policy toward home and community-based services. In *Olmstead*, the Court ruled that the unnecessary segregation of individuals in long-term care facilities constitutes discrimination under the Americans with Disabilities Act (ADA). States are required, when it is appropriate and reasonable to do so, to serve individuals with disabilities in community settings rather than in institutions. The Court directed each state to develop a comprehensive, effective working plan to place qualified individuals in less restrictive settings and to assure that people come off waiting lists at a reasonable pace.

Olmstead affects those at risk of institutionalization as well as those currently institutionalized. Therefore, any reform efforts brought on by the decision must involve changes not only to the long-term provision of public health services (primarily Medicaid) but also to housing, transportation and other fundamental support services that are essential to fully integrate individuals with disabilities into least restrictive settings.

Community-Based Case System Is Badly Needed

A comprehensive national policy that shifts the focus *and* funding of long-term care to community-based services is essential to meet the needs and address the desires of America's aging population. Independence, dignity and choice are strongly held values by all Americans, and individuals with physical or cognitive limitations and impairments are no exception. By shifting national policies toward home and community-based services, the quality of life of older adults will improve, taxpayers will be spared the cost of premature and expensive institutional care, and our nation's core values will be honored.

> *A comprehensive national policy that shifts the focus* and *funding of long-term care to community-based services is essential.*

A sound home and community-based system of long-term care provides a coordinated and broad range of services that address the medical, social and environmental needs of the individual. . . . The following principles must be adhered to for a home and community-based system to best meet the needs of those it serves, including the not-too-distant future needs of the baby boomer generation.

Reform Medicaid. Medicaid, the largest public program financing long-term care, has an inherent bias toward institutionalization. Congress established the home and community-based service waiver in 1981 to attempt to reduce this bias. The Medicaid waiver program gives states the option to apply for waivers to fund home and community-based services for people who meet Medicaid eligibility requirements for nursing home care. A recent study by the Assistant Secretary for Planning and Evaluation with the U.S. Department of Health and Human Services found that average spending on the aged and disabled under the Medicaid home and community-based waiver saved money—providing for an individual under the waiver program costs $5,820 a year compared to $29,112 for nursing home care. Even so, nursing home care remains a basic service under Medicaid, while states still face a burdensome waiver process to offer home and community-based services.

> *❝ By shifting national priorities toward home and community-based services, the quality of life of older adults will improve. ❞*

Build Upon the Successes of the Older Americans Act. The Older Americans Act (OAA) has been the foundation of services for older adults throughout the country since its enactment in 1965 and forms the nucleus of a national system of home and community-based services. OAA funds, and the services they make possible, are augmented by leveraging state and local government funding, as well as private sector, foundation, participant and volunteer contributions. OAA funding has not kept pace with inflation or the growing population of individuals eligible for services. Significant increases in federal appropriations are crucial to assure the availability of services and programs that enhance the ability of older Americans to live with maximum independence.

Enhance Support for Family Caregivers. The majority of people of all ages with chronic disabling conditions rely on family members or friends as their primary source of care. Nearly one out of every four households (23 percent or 22.4 million households) is involved in caregiving to persons age 50 or older. Among older adults with long-term care needs, nearly 95 percent receive some or all of their care from informal caregivers who often suffer emotional, physical and financial hardships as a result of caregiving. Furthermore, cultural and demographic changes are reducing the pool of available caregivers just as the baby boomer generation approaches retirement age. The National Family Caregiver Support Program, enacted in 2000 as part of the Older Americans Act reauthorization, and numerous state programs provide support services for caregivers, but current federal funding is insufficient to meet caregiver needs.

Link Affordable Housing with Needed Support Services. Housing security is critical to the health and well being of older adults. The home and community-based system will not succeed without the provision of affordable and accessible housing for older adults. Greater coordination needs to occur between housing and service providers to guarantee that support services, such as meals, personal assistance and housekeeping, as well as health services, are readily available and easily obtainable. While policy initiatives are underway to increase existing assisted living facilities stock, convert existing public housing into accessible housing, and provide increased coordination of support and housing services, progress has been slow and more commitment to these efforts by policymakers is needed.

Develop Systems to Help Older Adults Retain Mobility. Mobility is essential for an individual to live at home and in the community. Transportation provides necessary access to medical care, shopping for daily essentials and the ability to participate in cultural, recreational and religious activities. Feelings of isolation and loss have been reported among older adults who can no longer use personal automobiles. Public policy must focus on the provision of safe, reliable and convenient alternative means of transportation for those for whom driving is no longer an option, as well as on efforts to help older adults retain their licenses and cars for as long as possible.

> *Medicaid, the largest public program financing long-term care, has an inherent bias toward institutionalization.*

Design Responsive Mental Health Services. Good mental health is fundamental to the well being of older adults and has a major impact on quality of life and optimal functioning. Yet, as the U.S. Surgeon General's 1999 report on mental health points out, too many older adults struggle with mental disorders that compromise their ability to participate fully in life. Older adults underutilize mental health services, for both social and systemic reasons, and care professionals and social services personnel frequently fail to recognize the signs and symptoms of mental illness. Service gaps, lack of collaboration among service agencies, and shortages of trained personnel also contribute to a poorly functioning mental health service system. Policymakers must work toward resolving current challenges in the design and delivery of mental health services that affect quality of life for the older population.

Expand Nutrition and Wellness Programs. Good nutrition and daily physical activity both play important roles in preventing or forestalling the onset of chronic conditions as well as reducing the effects of existing conditions. Nutrition programs such as congregate and home-delivered meals, provided through the Older Americans Act and other government programs, not only improve participants' dietary intake but also provide a social outlet for older adults at risk of isolation. Unfortunately, long waiting lists for these meals programs exist throughout the country. And while fewer structured programs exist to promote physical activity, the social, economic and health benefits of daily exercise must be recognized. Greater emphasis needs to be placed on the development and expansion of programs that promote sound nutrition and increased physical activity at the federal, state and local level.

Increase Efforts to Prevent Elder Abuse and Neglect. The dependence on others for care and assistance whether at home or in a facility leaves older adults, especially the most frail, vulnerable to abuse, neglect and exploitation. Adult protective services are designed to reduce the incidence of abuse and neglect and are essential to making it possible for older adults to remain safely in their homes and communities. Many older adult victims do not report abuse and many cases are not prosecuted. Staffing shortages, poor training and heavy caseloads contribute to unsatisfactory protective services. Greater outreach and educational efforts and increased collaboration among service providers at the federal, state and local level are important measures that can be taken to prevent and decrease all types of elder abuse.

Collaborate on Solutions to Workforce Shortages. At a time when an increasing percentage of the population needs direct care services, our nation is facing a serious shortage of workers in this industry. Paraprofessional personnel shortages can be attributed to, among other things, low pay, inadequate employee benefits including lack of health insurance, insufficient training and minimal chance for career advancement. Moreover, health care agencies have a hard time maintaining employees due primarily to poor reimbursement rates from both public (Medicare, Medicaid) and private providers. Furthermore, the care that is provided by these workers is undervalued by society. Policymakers need to work collaboratively with workers unions, service providers and consumers to recruit and retain a stable, reliable workforce.

7

The Government Must Increase Funding for Alzheimer's Research and Care

Stephen McConnell

Stephen McConnell is senior vice president of advocacy and public policy for the Alzheimer's Association, a nonprofit organization dedicated to eradicating Alzheimer's disease.

Alzheimer's disease may be the biggest epidemic of the twenty-first century. An estimated 4.5 million Americans currently have Alzheimer's, a progressive disease that dramatically impairs memory and is ultimately fatal. Over the next fifty years that number is expected to reach 16 million as the baby boom generation ages. The financial cost of Alzheimer's is staggering, and caring for those who have the disease is extremely demanding. The federal government should increase funding for Alzheimer's research in order to find a cure or a way to prevent Alzheimer's and to improve the lives of those who already have the disease.

Editor's Note: Stephen McConnell presented the following testimony to the U.S. Senate Special Committee on Aging on April 27, 2004.

The growing epidemic of Alzheimer's disease is generating catastrophic human and economic costs to American society and to societies around the world. The goal of the Alzheimer's

Stephen McConnell, testimony before the U.S. Senate Special Committee on Aging, Washington, DC, April 27, 2004.

Association, working in partnership with government and private industry, is to eradicate this disease. Through these combined efforts of the Association, National Institutes of Health, and the pharmaceutical industry, advances in medical treatment have surged forward in recent years.

> *Caring for persons with Alzheimer's disease takes an enormous toll on the U.S. healthcare system.*

In the meantime, we must improve diagnosis, treatment and care; support family caregivers; address human resource challenges in the delivery of health care services; and improve care in facilities, at home, and in communities, whether rural, suburban or urban. We must do this in cost-effective ways that enhance quality of life for individuals, families and caregivers.

These are no small challenges, but technology provides enormous opportunities for addressing them. The Alzheimer's Association has assumed a leadership role by investing significant resources in exploring these technologies. . . . In addition, the Alzheimer's Association recently announced that more than 150 local, state and national organizations representing more than 50 million Americans have come together to form the "Coalition of Hope"—the largest coalition ever organized to support increased funding for research to find new treatments to help those with Alzheimer's disease. . . .

Federal Government Should Play a Role

While much of the developmental work in technology is being carried out by private sector organizations, the Alzheimer's Association believes there is a definite role for the federal government. In addition to continued oversight, a key role is to bring stakeholders together in order to draw attention to the issues and give impetus to developmental efforts. A national commission on technology and aging, with special emphasis on those with cognitive impairment, should be created to focus public and private attention and resources on addressing these issues. A series of additional hearings should be convened to provide oversight on progress, to stimulate interest among various stakeholders, and to identify policy impediments to implementation of technological solutions.

Other roles for the federal government include supporting research on assistive technology in partnership with private industry and voluntary health agencies like the Alzheimer's Association. In addition, emphasis should be placed on continuing and increasing federal funding for Alzheimer's disease research to maintain the momentum of advanced understanding of the causes and potential treatments of the disease while also seeking to find solutions for improving the care of those already diagnosed with the disease.

The Growing Alzheimer's Epidemic

The challenges posed by Alzheimer's disease affect this country at a personal, an economic, and a societal level. An estimated 4.5 million Americans currently have Alzheimer's disease. Increasing age is the greatest risk factor for Alzheimer's. One in ten individuals over age 65 and nearly half over 85 are affected. The number of Americans with Alzheimer's will continue to grow as our population ages and life expectancy rates soar. By 2050, Alzheimer's could affect anywhere from 11.3 million to 16 million people.

Alzheimer's Costs Are Skyrocketing

Caring for persons with Alzheimer's disease takes an enormous toll on the U.S. healthcare system. At any particular time, approximately 20 percent (1.1 million) of persons with Alzheimer's are in nursing homes and between five and ten percent (450,000–600,000) are in assisted living facilities. By 2010, Medicare costs for beneficiaries with Alzheimer's are expected to increase nearly 55 percent, from $31.9 billion in 2000 to $49.3 billion and Medicaid expenditures on residential dementia care will increase 80 percent, from $18.2 billion to $33 billion. Nearly half (49 percent) of Medicare beneficiaries who have Alzheimer's disease also receive Medicaid. The average annual cost of Alzheimer care in a nursing home is $64,000.

Medicaid pays nearly half of the total nursing home bill and helps two out of three residents pay for their care. Alzheimer's disease costs American business $61 billion annually, $36.5 billion of which is caused by the lost productivity of employees who are caregivers. Utilizing assistive technologies to prolong a person's ability to live independently, thus reducing the need for expensive institutional care, has the potential to save billions of dollars in Medicare and Medicaid spending, as well as family budgets.

Caregiving Is Demanding Work

Caring for persons with Alzheimer's also places a heavy burden on the families and friends of those with the disease. Alzheimer caregiving is intense, hard, and exhausting work. Seventy percent of people with Alzheimer's live at home, where family and friends provide the majority of their care. Alzheimer caregivers devote more time to the day-to-day tasks of caring and they provide help with greater numbers of activities of daily living (including incontinence, one of the biggest challenges of caregiving). One in eight Alzheimer caregivers becomes ill or injured as a direct result of caregiving and one in three uses medications for problems related to caregiving.

Older caregivers are three times more likely to become clinically depressed than others in their age group and one study found that elderly spouses strained by caregiving were 63 percent more likely to die during a four-year period than other spouses their age. Assistive devices that allow individuals with cognitive impairments to complete activities of daily living with less dependence on their caregivers is one area in which technology may help alleviate some of the fatigue and "caregiver burnout" faced by loved ones of individuals with Alzheimer's disease.

> *Utilizing assistive technologies to prolong a person's ability to live independently, thus reducing the need for expensive institutional care, has the potential to save billions of dollars.*

The caregiving challenges presented by Alzheimer's disease extend to the long term care workforce as well. Today more than 1 million nursing assistants provide as much as 90 percent of hands-on care in nursing homes and other settings. The Bureau of Labor Statistics estimates that by 2006, personal home and care aides are projected to be the fourth-fastest growing occupation, with a dramatic 84.7 percent growth rate expected. Despite the growth in the industry and the increased demand for talented workers, there is a long term care workforce crisis. National long term care staff turnover rates are at an alarming 94 percent annually.

Better Training Is Needed

Numerous issues contribute to this crisis including insufficient staff, low wages, inadequate benefits, lack of dementia-specific training, little or no job recognition and few career advancement opportunities. Staffing shortages affect the overall quality of care to residents and contribute directly to staff turnover. One of the most important steps toward improving the quality of care is better training. Certified Nursing Assistants surveyed in a 1999 Iowa Caregiver's Association report indicated that their work was increasingly demanding and complex and that they needed more training and orientation. Respondents specifically mentioned the importance of Alzheimer's training and understanding behaviors related to dementia. With up to 16 million people expected to develop Alzheimer's disease by the middle of the 21st century, nearly all of whom will eventually require total care, a solution to the workforce crisis must be found immediately. Technology that can be used to provide ongoing, interactive training for staff in long term care facilities is one part of the solution to the broader workforce problem.

Symptoms and Signs of Alzheimer's

Individuals living with Alzheimer's disease face challenges at all stages of the disease. Common symptoms at the beginning and moderate stages are impaired memory, judgment, and reasoning ability. As Alzheimer's progresses, individuals with the disease may lose the ability to manage their own health care, may not be able to follow medication instructions, and may need frequent cueing or reminders when completing routine tasks. All are likely at some point in the disease process to require 24-hour supervision and assistance. Individuals with Alzheimer's may also experience difficult or challenging behavior problems that lead to violent episodes, an issue explored by this committee in a hearing just last month [March 2004]. Several population-based studies have found that upwards of 90 percent of people with dementia develop one or more psychiatric and related behavioral problems. Wandering is another common and potentially life-threatening behavior associated with Alzheimer's disease. Studies report wandering in 4 to 26 percent of nursing home residents with dementia and in up to 59 percent of community-residing individuals suffering from the disease. Utilizing existing technology, such as electronic monitoring devices, may provide solutions to the everyday challenges faced by individuals with Alzheimer's disease.

Technology Can Play a Key Role in Care

Technological innovations have enormous potential to address some of the challenges posed by Alzheimer's disease. Through our partnership with The Center for Aging Services Technologies (CAST), the Alzheimer's Association is working to identify how technology can improve Alzheimer's care and services. CAST has identified four areas where technology might improve aging services—providing ways to improve independence and allow people to remain independent longer (enabling); addressing the human resources and productivity issues of aging services providers (operational); improving the connections between individuals and their families and social support networks (connective); and dealing with geographic barriers to good care (telemedicine). These focus areas coincide with key priority areas for Alzheimer's care.

> *With up to 16 million people expected to develop Alzheimer's disease by the middle of the 21st century, nearly all of whom will eventually require total care, a solution to the workforce crisis must be found immediately.*

An example of enabling technology that may help prolong independent living is a "Smart House" that includes features such as stoves with automatic cutoff devices and kitchen heat sensors to prevent fires. "Smart Houses" may also include devices that cue and remind individuals with Alzheimer's disease to take medications or help them locate lost possessions. In addition, Artificial Intelligence is being tested to help individuals with Alzheimer's disease complete activities of daily living with less dependence on their caregivers.

Promoting safety is another major concern of the Alzheimer's Association. A wide variety of electronic tracking devices are currently available to monitor, track and locate individuals with Aizheimer's disease who wander. . . .

Telemedicine has the potential to reduce geographic barriers to good care. Telehealth and telemedicine technologies are being assessed for possible use in providing supervision (including monitoring sleep and eating patterns and medication compliance/accuracy) of individuals with Alzheimer's who live alone.

Success Requires a Team Effort

Developing, testing and measuring the viability and feasibility of various technologies to improve care and promote healthy aging requires collaboration among technology companies, researchers, service providers and advocacy organizations. Meeting the distinct needs of the aging population, particularly those with Alzheimer's disease, will require a complex, multidimensional approach. . . .

In recent years, while advances in treatments for brief symptomatic relief have surged forward, progress in improving services and technologies for routine care of people with prolonged disability and loss of independent functioning have lagged behind. Delaying and eventually preventing cognitive impairments could have far greater significance for the economics of health and well being than providing short-term, symptomatic relief. . . .

Public Policy Issues

There are a variety of public policy aspects, especially around reimbursement and regulatory issues, that may influence the broader development and adoption of assistive technologies for seniors and individuals with Alzheimer's disease. For example, alternative treatment models using telemedicine to help manage care for persons with Alzheimer's disease in rural areas might be very successful, but these models are not currently reimbursable, or reimbursement is very cumbersome. Determining how to measure the practical and care outcomes of using technology, conducting additional research to assess whether technology can reduce the cost of care or increase caregiver efficiency, and promoting more widespread use of existing technology in various care settings are just a few of the challenges faced by this burgeoning field. It will be necessary for government and private industry to examine all public policies, including possible Medicare and Medicaid reimbursement, to determine the impact on the development, adoption and use of technology. . . .

Technology Poses Challenges Too

Efforts to incorporate the use of technology more broadly in the care of persons with cognitive impairments such as Alzheimer's disease pose some unique challenges for caregivers in all settings. These challenges include:

• Adapting existing technologies so that they can be utilized by people with cognitive impairments.

• Determining the applicability of existing technologies in various Alzheimer's care settings.

• Considering the ethical issues related to use of technology, such as obtaining consent, maintaining privacy rights and preserving decision-making autonomy for individuals with cognitive impairments.

• Responding to cultural, language and ethnicity issues, both in how people will react to technology and to ensure technology is diffused into communities in ways that are culturally appropriate.

• Developing models that integrate human aspects with technology to deliver high quality care with greater efficiency.

All of these issues can be addressed, and while they address issues specific to people with cognitive impairments, they are important to everyone who will be using or be affected by technology in care settings. . . .

As was acknowledged earlier, much of the developmental work in technology is being carried out by private sector organizations the Alzheimer's Association believes the federal government can play a role in this area by:

• Creating a national commission on technology and aging, with a special emphasis on those with cognitive impairments, to focus public and private attention and resources on addressing these issues.

• Supporting research on assistive technology in partnership with private industry and voluntary health agencies like the Alzheimer's Association.

• Convening a series of additional hearings to provide oversight on progress, to stimulate interest among various stakeholders and to identify policy impediments to implementation of technological solutions.

• Continuing and increasing federal funding for Alzheimer's disease research to maintain the momentum of advanced understanding of the causes and potential treatments of the disease while also seeking to find solutions for improving the care of those already diagnosed with the disease.

Entering a New Era

We have entered a new era in the fight against Alzheimer's disease. Over the last twenty years we have gone from hopeless to hopeful and are at the point where the goal of a world without Aizheimer's disease is within reach. Working collaboratively, the federal government, the scientific community, the Alzheimer's Association and the pharmaceutical industry have made tremendous progress in the prevention, diagnosis and treatment of Alzheimer's disease. Even with the progress that has been made, we still face many challenges, especially in delivering healthcare services and improving care for individuals with Alzheimer's disease in facilities, at home and in communities. These are big challenges but technology provides enormous opportunities for addressing them.

The Alzheimer's Association has assumed a leadership role by investing significant resources in exploring these technologies through the creation of a Technology Workgroup, by launching with Intel Corporation the Everyday Technologies for Alzheimer's Care consortium, and by joining the Center for Aging Services Technologies commission sponsored by the American Association of Homes & Services for the Aging. While much of the developmental work in technology is being carried out by private sector organizations, it is essential that the federal government intervene to enable both sectors to focus more attention and resources on this promising area. We are committed to working with you and all of our partner organizations to shape a future in which technology will improve the lives of people with chronic conditions like Alzheimer's disease, as well as the lives of their caregivers and families.

8

The Government Must Provide Transportation Programs for Seniors Who Cannot Drive

Larry Lipman

Larry Lipman covers aging issues as a senior reporter with Cox News Service, a newspaper wire service.

For most elderly people, being able to drive a car is an important part of their independence. However, many seniors continue driving longer than they safely should because they do not want to give up their freedom or because they fear imposing on family or friends to take them places. Every year, about eight hundred thousand senior citizens in the United States give up driving—but they still need to go places. More government funding is needed for transportation programs for seniors, especially because the number of nondrivers will grow so rapidly over the next thirty years.

Jane Tuttle quit driving the day a routine shopping trip turned terrifying. Alone and needing to get home, Tuttle, 81, discovered she was unable to feel the difference between the gas and brake pedals because of a medical condition that can cause numbness in the feet. She made it home that day without incident, but after 65 years of driving she gave her car keys to her son. "It's been a big shock to find myself without wheels. It's terrible. You are totally dependent," Tuttle said.

Larry Lipman, "America Facing a Crisis of Elderly Non-Drivers," Cox News Service, April 13, 2004.

Fears of isolation or loss of independence keep many elderly people behind the wheel beyond the time it's safe. But as America ages, it will inevitably face a transportation crisis for those who no longer drive.

Country Is Not Prepared

It's a crisis for which the nation has made few preparations. Older non-drivers are reluctant to impose on friends, who often have their own driving difficulties. Walking and public transportation are usually not adequate options, and the idea of community-based transportation networks for the elderly are just starting to take root.

The problem is growing quickly. An estimated 800,000 elderly people quit driving in the United States each year. Millions more limit the time of day, the type of roads, or the distance they travel. Already, more than 7 million Americans over 65—one in five—are non-drivers, according to the U.S. Department of Transportation. . . . The average age at which elderly drivers quit is about 85, according to Daniel J. Foley, an epidemiologist at the National Institute on Aging. Currently, about 7 million Americans are 85 and older. That will increase to about 9 million by 2030, when the oldest of today's baby boomers hit their mid-80s, and will nearly triple to 19 million by 2050.

Most people can expect to live for many years after they've quit driving. A study led by Foley determined that on average, elderly women live another 10 years, and men live another seven years, after they stop driving.

Losing Driving Privilege Is Traumatic

Public attention has been focused on making sure that elderly drivers are safe on the road, such as Florida's law this year [2004] requiring vision screening for all drivers 80 or older when they renew their license. Other efforts have been aimed at making it easier for elderly drivers to continue driving—by making road signs more visible, building separate left-turn lanes and improving car technology to make information such as directions more available. But there has been little focus on what happens when people can no longer drive.

"We have far to go in thinking what to do with these people now that we've taken their independence, their self-esteem, their self-worth and said: 'You're a danger, you can't drive any more,'" said Stella Henry, founder and director of the Vista del Sol Care Center, a long-term care facility in Culver City, Calif.

"Going grocery shopping, going to the cleaners, visiting a friend, the grandchild, or simply just getting out for a cup of bad coffee is what life is about," said Joseph Coughlin, director of the Massachusetts Institute of Technology's AgeLab.

> **//** *The average age at which elderly drivers quit is about 85.* **//**

Many former drivers become virtual prisoners in their homes, experts say. Typical is Jerry Gismondi, of Boca Raton, Fla., who quit driving two decades ago and relies on a local senior center bus to go to the center and grocery store. The 75-year-old misses going out for an evening movie or the symphony because of a lack of late-night public transportation. Taxis are too expensive, he said, and he's reluctant to ask friends. "I feel embarrassed," he said.

Non-Drivers Experience Isolation

A recent report by the Surface Transportation Policy Project, a nonprofit coalition of groups interested in promoting safe communities and transportation alternatives, found that:

• More than half of non-drivers over 65 stay home on any given day, citing a lack of transportation options.

• Compared with elderly drivers, elderly non-drivers make 15 percent fewer doctor trips, 60 percent fewer shopping and dining trips, and 65 percent fewer trips for social, family and religious activities.

• Non-driving is more common in minority communities. While about 16 percent of elderly whites do not drive, 39 percent of older Latinos, 42 percent of blacks and 45 percent of Asian-Americans do not drive.

For many older non-drivers, options are limited. Once they give up driving, many elderly rely on family and friends to drive them. But family members may not live nearby, or may find it a strain to provide transportation in the middle of a workday. Friends may be roughly the same age as the former driver and barely able to drive themselves. Friendships might be strained by relying on another person for a ride, particularly if it involves a lengthy wait at a doctor's office for example. When that happens, an elderly person may feel "so embarrassed . . . they don't feel like they can get a ride with them again because they feel they have taken up such a big hunk of that person's time," said Jon E. Burkhardt, a senior study director at WESTAT, a Rockville, Md., research group. "Sometimes it's hard for older folks to pay back a favor like 'take me to the doctors' office,' particularly if that takes three or four hours."

Public Transportation Poses Hardship

Experts say public transportation is not the answer. With the population shift out of the cities since World War II, more than half of America's elderly live in the suburbs, and another quarter live in rural areas, far from public transportation. Even those who do live near public transportation may be unable to use it. The same physical and mental health problems that often lead people to quit driving make it difficult for them to use public transportation. A bus stop several blocks away may be too far for an elderly person to walk, particularly in snow and ice. Waiting for a bus in the heat also may be too difficult for many. Bus steps can be difficult to navigate and bus schedules can tax the memories of those with varying degrees of dementia. More than that, experts say, people who have spent most of their lives driving are not likely to begin taking the bus in their old age. "You don't wake up at 75 and say, 'You know, I think I'll take the bus,'" Coughlin said.

> *You don't wake up at 75 and say, 'You know, I think I'll take the bus.'*

Use of public transit nationally by the elderly has been steadily declining. In 1995, the elderly used public transit for a scant 2.2 percent of their trips. By 2001, that percentage had dropped to a minuscule 1.3 percent, according to Sandra Rosenbloom, director of the Roy P. Drachman Institute for Land and Regional Development Studies at the University of Arizona in a paper written for the Brookings Institution.

Seniors Need More Options

While most large communities have alternative transportation services beyond the fixed-route public transit lines, many of them have severe limits on when they will operate, where they will go, and who is eligible to ride. "Community services, religious groups, etc., have defined the transportation needs of the elderly as basically going to the doctor, grocery or religious activity," Coughlin said. "Real life is about more than going to the drug store and going to the doctor's office." Although more than half of elderly Americans say they walk regularly, it is often not a viable alternative to driving. And while walking, in general, is good for the health, it can be dangerous as a means of transportation. "Older people are much more endangered as pedestrians than they are as drivers or car passengers," Rosenbloom said in an interview, noting the dangers of elderly people slipping on ice, leaves or tripping over roots in the sidewalk.

Some communities have encouraged the elderly to use alternative vehicles such as motorized golf carts to get around, but Rosenbloom said not enough planning has gone into making them a viable solution, even in "planned" communities where a retail hub is surrounded by neighborhoods. She said the same problems older drivers may experience may prevent them from operating alternative vehicles.

Funding Programs Should Be a Priority

In a few places, alternative transportation programs have been provided at the local level, but federal support for such programs is limited. The federal government has provided financial aid to private organizations such as agencies on aging, the American Red Cross and United Way to purchase vans and mini-buses to bring people to their facilities. The last six-year transportation bill, which expires this year [in 2004], authorized $456 million for the program. Both the House and Senate versions of the new bill increase that funding.

Transportation assistance for the elderly "has been a cobbled-together investment of reports, events and demonstration projects," Coughlin said. "Quite frankly, we are losing time. It takes years to change infrastructure, it takes decades to change living patterns. Even if we were to act today with a coherent policy and with a real commitment," he said. "By the time the oldest group (of boomers) reaches 75, 80 years old, unless somebody puts transportation on the agenda, we're not going to make it."

9

Society Must Confront Ageism and Discrimination

David Crary

David Crary writes on national issues for the Associated Press, a newspaper wire service.

Society is rife with negative images and stereotypes about aging, and seniors frequently encounter age discrimination on the job and in health care settings. Cultural attitudes about getting old play a major part in how elderly people are treated in society as well as in how seniors view themselves. Attitudes about getting old may even affect how long a person lives. Many experts agree that society must work to eliminate ageism so that old age is once again respected rather than reviled.

Greeting-card and novelty companies call them "Over the Hill" products: the 50th Birthday Coffin Gift Boxes featuring prune juice and anti-aging soap; the "Old Coot" and "Old Biddy" bobblehead dolls; the birthday cards mocking the mobility, intellect and sex drive of the no-longer-young.

Many Americans chuckle at such humor. Others see it as offensive, as one more sign of pervasive ageism in America.

It's a bias some also see in substandard conditions at nursing homes, in pension-plan cutbacks by employers, in the relative invisibility of the elderly on television shows and in advertisements.

"Daily we are witness to, or even unwitting participants in, cruel imagery, jokes, language, and attitudes directed at older people," contends Dr. Robert Butler, president of the International Longevity Center–USA and the person who coined the term "ageism" 35 years ago.

That ageism exists, in a society captivated by youth culture and taut-skinned good looks, is scarcely debatable. But as the oldest of the 77 million baby boomers approach their 60s, the elderly and their concerns will inevitably move higher on the national agenda.

Will Ageism Get Worse or Better?

Already, there is lively debate as to whether ageism will ease or grow worse in the coming decades of boomer senior citizenship. Erdman Palmore, a professor emeritus at Duke University who has written or edited more than a dozen books on aging, counts himself—cautiously—among the optimists.

"One can say unequivocally that older people are getting smarter, richer and healthier as time goes on," Palmore said. "I've dedicated most of my life to combating ageism, and it's tempting for me to see it everywhere. . . . But I have faith that as science progresses, and reasonable people get educated about it, we will come to recognize ageism as the evil it is."

Palmore, 74, lives what he preaches—challenging the stereotypes of aging by skydiving, whitewater rafting, bicycling his age in miles each birthday. He recently got a tattoo on his shoulder, though the image he chose was the relatively discreet symbol of the American Humanist Association.

> **❝**Daily we are witness to, or even unwitting participants in, cruel imagery, jokes, language, and attitudes directed at older people.**❞**

"What makes me mad is how aging, in our language and culture, is equated with deterioration and impairment," Palmore said. "I don't know how we're going to root that out, except by making people more aware of it."

To the extent that ageism persists, there will soon be many more potential targets. The number of Americans 65 and older is projected to double over the next three decades from 35.9

million to nearly 70 million, comprising 20 percent of the population in 2030 compared to less than 13 percent now.

The 85-and-over population is the fastest growing segment —projected to grow from 4 million in 2000 to 19 million in 2050 as part of an unprecedented surge in longevity. Americans now turning 65 will live, on average, an additional 18 years.

Ageism May Affect Longevity

Some researchers believe that ageism, in the form of negative stereotypes, directly affects longevity. In a study published by the American Psychological Association, Yale School of Public Health professor Becca Levy and her colleagues concluded that old people with positive perceptions of aging lived an average of 7.5 years longer than those with negative images of growing older.

Levy said many Americans start developing stereotypes about the elderly during childhood, reinforce them throughout adulthood, and enter old age with attitudes toward their own age group as unfavorable as younger people's attitudes.

"It's possible to overcome the stereotypes, but they often operate without people's awareness," Levy said. "Look at all the talk about plastic surgery, Botox—the message is, 'Don't get old.'"

Age Discrimination on the Job

For thousands of American workers, it's the same message they claim to hear on the job. The U.S. Equal Employment Opportunity Commission [EEOC] has received more than 19,000 age discrimination complaints in each of the past two years, and has helped win tens of millions of dollars in settlements.

However, attorneys say age discrimination often is hard to prove. Only about one-seventh of the EEOC age cases were settled to the complainant's benefit.

New Yorker Bill DeLong, 84, was fired three years ago from his longtime job as a waiter at a Shea Stadium restaurant, but he continues to seek out charitable volunteer assignments and still works as a waiter occasionally at special events.

"I didn't give up," he said. "A lot of my contemporaries give up too soon."

Seventy-eight-year-old Catherine Roberts stays active with New York City's Joint Public Affairs Committee for Older Adults,

a coalition that encourages seniors to advocate on their own behalf on legislative and community issues.

"I don't have time to get old," said Roberts, who came to
New York from Maine in 1955. "I'm too busy."

Yet despite her upbeat outlook, she resents how some of her
peers are treated. "We're a culture that worships youth," she
said. "Seniors are getting pushed aside. I see people in my building whose families ignore them—they fall through the cracks."

Elders Face Ageism in Health Care

For many older people, ageism surfaces most painfully in the
context of health care. A report by the Alliance for Aging Research, presented to a Senate committee last year [2003], said
the elderly are less likely to receive preventive care and often
lack access to doctors trained in their needs.

Only about 10 percent of U.S. medical schools require work
in geriatric medicine. The American Geriatrics Society says
there are only about 7,600 physicians nationwide certified as
geriatric specialists—not enough to meet demand and far be-
low the 36,000 the society says will be needed by 2030.

While the society says the best way to attract more doctors
to the field is to make Medicare practice more lucrative, some
experts believe that many medical students also have negative
attitudes toward the elderly that should be challenged.

In one such effort, the National Institute on Aging, working with Johns Hopkins Medical School and a Baltimore mu-
seum, teamed elderly people and first-year medical students in
an art program in which they drew, made collages, sang songs
and shared stories. A survey showed the students gained a more
positive view of seniors and of geriatrics as a possible specialty.

Advertisers Cater to Young Market

Ageism also manifests itself in advertising. Though adults of all
ages drink beer and buy cars, for example, TV and print ads for
those products almost invariably feature youthful actors and
models.

According to AARP, the lobbying group for people 50 and
over, Americans in that age bracket account for half of all consumer spending but are targeted by just 10 percent of marketing. The dynamic is particularly potent in television, where
network executives gear programming toward 18-to-34-year-

olds because advertisers will pay more to reach those viewers. "When an older person sees a product targeted to a younger person, they're willing to buy it, but young people will not buy a product targeted to an older person," said Jim Fishman, group publisher for AARP Publications.

Fishman, who oversees AARP's three magazines, predicts advertisers will increasingly tilt their messages toward older consumers as the baby boomers enter their 60s.

"By and large, the wealth that resides in the older segment of the population is disposable wealth—the kids are done with college, the mortgage is paid off," Fishman said. "This older market is huge and feeling largely ignored."

Attitudes on Aging Are Changing

Looking ahead, Fishman foresees people of all ages, elderly included, gaining the ability to look more attractive than in the past thanks to developments ranging from Botox to fitness programs. He also expects a more deep-rooted change in society's view of aging as the 65-and-older ranks are filled with increasing numbers of computer-savvy boomers, eager for civic engagement and lifelong education programs.

> *There will always be people in society who can't come to terms with other people's aging because they can't come to terms with their own aging.*

Still, David Wolfe, whose book *Ageless Marketing* advises advertisers how to reach over-50 consumers, says ageism is likely to persist. "There will always be people in society who can't come to terms with other people's aging because they can't come to terms with their own aging," he said.

Paul Kleyman, editor of the American Society on Aging's bimonthly newspaper, has testified before Congress that ageism is common in the mass media. He tells of a magazine editor who wanted fewer stories about "prune faces," and of a Chicago talk radio station whose staff was told to screen out "old-sounding" callers.

Kleyman also detects some positive trends, including a growing number of newspapers assigning reporters to cover aging-related issues on a regular basis.

"The drive in the news industry is for younger readers, but don't just ignore the loyal older readers you have," he said. "We should be encouraging society to be receptive to a more active older generation, instead of looking at boomers as a burden that's going to drain the nation."

The Young and the Old Compete for Resources

The short-term future of ageism may depend in large part on that question—whether or not baby boomers are viewed by younger Americans as a rival for economic resources and political clout as Society Security and Medicare costs rise.

> *The tens of millions of boomers will find that ageism is a unique form of bias in that it's universal—potentially affecting all who live long enough.*

"At the individual level of how people are treated, negative ageism is probably going to decline a little," said Robert Binstock, professor of aging and public policy at Case Western Reserve School of Medicine in Cleveland. "But at the societal level it's quite possible we'll see an increase in ageism, a sense of, 'Wow, what an unsustainable burden older people are going to be.'"

Bob Robinson, 88, of Aurora, Colo., a former director of services for the aging in Colorado, said he has encountered a generational gap while lobbying legislators on senior issues.

"The politicians consider that with Social Security and Medicare and the other advantages that seniors have, we're in pretty good shape," Robinson said. "It's true for a lot of us, but not for all of us. Many seniors worked for small businesses that had no retirement system."

Bobbie Sackman of New York City's Council of Senior Centers and Services agrees.

"Boomers are not all white, middle-class suburbanites," she said. "You will have the older people with greater resources, and that will in some ways change the image of aging. But you will also have those with less resources, coming from groups that already had faced discrimination, and now they will have the age thing added to the mix."

Boomers Will Shape Society's Attitudes

John Rother, policy director for the AARP, said the boomers, by their very numbers, are bound to change the public perception of aging.

"It will be more visible," he said. "People will survive longer, in better health. . . . They'll feel the market should cater to them, the political system should cater to them, as it has their whole lives."

Whatever their political clout, the tens of millions of boomers will find that ageism is a unique form of bias in that it's universal—potentially affecting all who live long enough.

"Everyone has a vested interest in eradicating this prejudice," wrote Richard Butler, the International Longevity Center president, in a recent briefing paper. "We all aspire to live to be old, and consequently we all must work to create a society where old age is respected, if not honored, and where persons who have reached old age are not marginalized."

10

The Elderly Must Be Protected from Abuse

Robert B. Blancato

Robert B. Blancato is the president of the National Committee to Prevent Elder Abuse (NCPEA), a nonprofit organization that promotes research, advocacy, and public awareness of elder justice issues.

Elder abuse can take many forms: physical, emotional, financial, or sexual. Seniors may be abused by family members or others in their homes, or in institutional settings such as nursing facilities. Seniors may also be victims of self-neglect if they cannot take care of themselves adequately. Although nearly half a million seniors are abused in the United States each year, government policy about the problem has been fragmented and ineffective. A comprehensive elder abuse policy is badly needed. Such a policy should increase adult protective services, train professionals, educate the public about elder abuse, and increase the prosecution of abusers. In February 2003, Senator John Breaux (D-LA) introduced the Elder Justice Act, a comprehensive bill that will make elder abuse the priority that it should be. In September 2004 the Senate Finance Committee approved the measure 20-0.

Elder abuse is not a new issue, but it has new urgency that compels some new approaches.

Statistically, based on the National Center on Elder Abuse's collection of data from states for the year including 2000, there were a total of 470,709 reports of adult/elder abuse. This represented a 60 percent increase from 1996. In addition, an esti-

Robert B. Blancato, statement before the U.S. Senate Committee on Finance, Washington, DC, June 18, 2002.

mated 15,000 complaints of abuse and gross neglect against older victims living in nursing homes and other long-term care facilities were reported, as well as 3500 similar complaints of abuse in board and care facilities.

Yet, estimates from the Senate Special Committee on Aging suggest the number of cases could be as many as 5 million, since more than eight out of every ten cases go unreported.

The federal involvement in elder abuse spans more than 23 years beginning with Congressional hearings before the House Select Committee on Aging. Eventually, federal programs were adopted and funding was provided for elder abuse prevention programs, adult protective services, and the Long-Term Care Ombudsman Program. This history includes the funding of a National Center on Elder Abuse, a Surgeon General's Report on Family Violence including elder abuse, and a National Elder Abuse Incidence Study. More recently, . . . the first National Summit on Elder Abuse was held under the auspices of the Administration on Aging and the Department of Justice in December 2001. We also note and commend the release of the National Academy of Sciences study on Risk and Prevalence of Elder Abuse and Neglect.

The reality is the federal response to combating elder abuse and neglect has been piecemeal and ultimately inadequate, as the problem has intensified. It is said in policy that sometimes it is all about money. If that criterion were applied, the current federal commitment pales even further. Consider that the only federal program that appropriates funds specifically addressed to elder abuse, Title VII of the Older Americans Act, has national funding of less than $5 million. It is estimated that the total federal commitment being spent today on programs addressing elder abuse, neglect and financial exploitation prevention is $153 million. This is all but .08 percent of the funds currently spent on abuse prevention programs whether for children, women or the elderly. It is not surprising, but is nonetheless disturbing, as Senator [John] Breaux [D-LA] recently noted, that there is not one single person working in the federal government full time on elder abuse prevention. . . .

Elder Justice Should Address Seven Goals

We need to move to a new approach in our fight against elder abuse, neglect and exploitation. Today our policies are more reactionary. Tomorrow they must be proactive, coordinated, comprehensive and goal driven. We suggest that a future elder justice policy could be built around the following seven goals addressed at the National Summit:

- Filling Service Gaps;
- Educating the Public;
- Training Professionals;
- Enhancing Adult Protective Services;
- Increasing Prosecution;
- Maximizing Resources; and
- Eliminating Policy Barriers.

NCPEA [National Committee to Prevent Elder Abuse] is proud to be working with Senator Breaux and his staff on his proposed Elder Justice Act. We believe the approach embodied in his proposal is the genuine catalyst that will shift the focus, change the direction and will move us from a federal response to a comprehensive policy on elder justice. We also believe it offers a strong balance in terms of the appropriate role of the federal government. Sometimes government is best when it supports and empowers. Sometimes its role is best when it is the engine developing and driving policy. Both will be needed here if we are to commit to a more serious and focused role of the federal government in elder justice.

> *The reality is the federal response to combating elder abuse and neglect has been piecemeal and ultimately inadequate, as the problem has intensified.*

We must first recognize that elder abuse is a public health, law enforcement and social services crisis. Therefore as a starting point, we must move from the current fragmentation and invisibility that exists within the federal government around elder abuse to one that is focused and will elevate elder justice as a priority.

Federal Government Must Show Leadership

The federal commitment to the future of elder justice must show leadership through responsibility, accountability, funding and visibility. One approach is offered in Senator Breaux's proposal. He would create Dual Offices of Elder Justice in both the Departments of Health and Human Services and the Department of Justice. This combined with a distinct federal home and a dedicated funding stream for Adult Protective Services is a major step in the right direction.

> **"** *The federal commitment to the future of elder justice must show leadership through responsibility, accountability, funding and visibility.* **"**

We must go beyond what is done inside the federal government in the new approach to elder justice. There must also be an entity created that represents the very valuable state, local, private and multidisciplinary perspectives that are working every day in the field of elder abuse prevention. This public-private entity could be charged with annually assessing the state of elder justice in our nation and could be the sponsoring entity of annual summits on elder justice.

Let me also add that important to any new and expanded federal commitment to elder justice must be regular Congressional oversight of existing and new programs and policies on elder justice to make them as coordinated as possible in the most cost effective manner.

The Need for Better Reporting

This new commitment to elder justice must absolutely include better data collection and dissemination. The underreporting of elder abuse, neglect and exploitation has several causes. Some are intensely personal relating to the victim. Others are intensely bureaucratic and must be remedied. We can begin by doing research in the areas of data and statistics, determine needs and costs, existing responsibilities and how best to measure outcomes.

As an example, the 15,000 cases of abuse in nursing homes mentioned above came from one source: the annual report of the Long-Term Care Ombudsman Program. It did not necessarily include reports that might have been submitted to state Medicare or Medicaid Fraud age agencies or state licensure or survey offices or even law enforcement. Why? Because there is no identifiable vehicle to collect, analyze or report this other data. This must be remedied. A new federal policy on elder justice must have the authority and the ability to achieve better reporting of abuse cases wherever it may occur.

The case for greater federal resources for elder justice is made much stronger with good data that justifies the need. We strongly believe that we must do more to identify, disseminate and utilize research being done today around elder abuse prevention. Further, where such research does not exist or if new areas of research should emerge, this new elder justice policy must commit dedicated new resources for research. Part of what should be in the research agenda is how to develop and track state-specific training outcomes, research on diverse populations relative to abuse and, something very critical, the development of uniform definitions and standardized reporting criteria. Good research is important for prevention of elder abuse neglect and financial exploitation and therefore is a good investment of federal money.

With respect to future research it is far wiser to sharpen the wheel than to reinvent it. Under a new elder justice policy we should do a basic inventory of what is being done in areas such as intervention, research or community strategies and other multi-disciplinary efforts and activities. These state and local models could be evaluated and recommended for possible national replication.

Extremely pivotal to the research agenda under a new elder justice policy must be a commitment to supporting regular national incidences and prevalence studies. These studies in so many ways could drive the elder justice policy as it could put researchers, front line workers and policymakers on the same page in terms of understanding the statistical extent of the problem as well as possible future trends.

Justice System Must Play a Primary Role

It is also important that a future elder justice policy support in different ways all the sectors involved in the fight against elder abuse and neglect. This is especially true for law enforcement. To achieve elder justice, the justice system needs to be made more aware of the elder abuse problem. As was noted at the National Summit, elder abuse and neglect must become a priority crime control issue. The justice system including law enforcement, prosecution, correct corrections, judiciary, medical examiners, coroners, public safety officers, victims advocates, APS [Adult Protective Services] workers and Ombudsman must work as a coordinated system to protect victims, hold offenders accountable and prevent future offenses.

In the future, there must also be an emphasis on training on an interdisciplinary, multidisciplinary and cross-educational basis. One of the suggestions from the Summit was a national elder abuse education and training curriculum that could be used by a variety of those involved in the field.

> ❝ To achieve elder justice, the justice system needs to be made more aware of the elder abuse problem. ❞

An obvious and critical goal in a future elder justice policy must be the goal of ensuring that elder abusers are never allowed to work in long-term care facilities or board and care facilities. This is a challenging and controversial issue that warrants deeper attention by Congress. Law enforcement must have the ability and tools to achieve swift prosecution against those who might already be employed, but commit abuse against an older person in the facility. In addition, some resources should be committed to training and educating of personnel in these facilities. In the book *Abuse Proofing Your Facility* (Pillemer), it is advanced that there are eight risk factors for someone to become an abuser in a facility; attitudes, burnout, conflict, disruptive/aggressive residents, education and training inadequacy, failure to enforce, gaps in staffing, hiring and screening deficiencies. The key point in this book is that these risk factors are all preventable. Let us commit more time and attention to this.

Consumers Need to Be Better Informed

We also need to enhance the knowledge base of consumers who are considering long-term care facilities for a loved one. This process to some extent has been started by CMS [the Centers for Medicare and Medicaid Services], but there must be much greater attention paid to distinguishing those facilities with clean records relative to abuse and those who have had problems in the past.

Today elder abuse is any form of mistreatment that results in harm or loss to an older person. It is generally divided into the following categories, yet a sad reality is there seem to be new categories appearing every day:

- Physical abuse;
- Sexual abuse;
- Domestic abuse (involving a family member);
- Psychological;
- Financial; and
- Neglect, including self-neglect.

Elder justice has individual and systemic definitions. From a policy perspective, elder justice consists of efforts to prevent, detect, treat, intervene in and, where appropriate, prosecute elder abuse, neglect and exploitation. From the individual perspective it is the right of older Americans to be free of abuse, neglect and exploitation.

> *To not direct the same level of commitment to elder abuse as to other abuse constitutes a new and deeply troubling form of ageism.*

We believe a new commitment to elder justice is as important as any initiative that has been undertaken to improve the quality of life for seniors in need. It reaffirms our commitment to the priority that federal policy has always given to those most vulnerable as older persons.

Elder Justice Act Has Far-Ranging Influence

The proposed Elder Justice Act has implications for a variety of programs and initiative, under this Committee's jurisdiction. Social Security is an example. Often it is the misappropriation of the monthly Social Security check by a relative that constitutes abuse. Medicare and Medicaid factor in through the new efforts to address quality of care and abuse prevention in long-term care facilities. This could be a key tool in reducing institutional-based elder abuse. On the other side of the coin is the victim of elder abuse, who may need extended acute care under Medicare to recover from the abuse and the demand that could cause on the program in the future. There is also support for having more Medicaid waiver programs offer community-based services for elder abuse prevention such as respite care. Any new elder justice policy will impact heavily on the Social Services Block Grant, which today is a main source of funding for adult protective services.

A new approach to elder justice could play into some future and pending tax bills including those that would provide incentives to recruit more qualified persons into healthcare, especially those who wish to specialize in geriatric medicine. In addition, as the Committee works further on caregiver legislation, elder justice and the need to provide assistance to caregivers to prevent abuse will come into play. Other areas that were presented at the summit for consideration are the establishment of a national toll-free number dealing with elder justice and a special Elder Justice awareness resolution.

The Public Must Be Educated About Elder Abuse

A new elder justice policy will rely on public-private partnerships. One area of this will be especially true: we need a sustained national strategic communication program to educate the public especially baby boomers and younger on elder abuse and elder justice. It will involve a national public awareness campaign on elder abuse. It must also work to apply pressure to prevent those occasional advertising campaigns that make light of issues around elder abuse such as exploitation. . . .

This elder justice proposal can also help to address key service gaps that exist today in elder abuse prevention. At the summit, mental health issues were identified as the top need in terms of filling service gaps. The summit called for appropriate and specialized mental health services to be available and accessible. Other service gaps commonly cited include preventive, early intervention and support services.

In closing, 29 years ago as a staffer in the House of Representatives, I worked with former Congressman Mario Biaggi and others including former Senator Walter Mondale on behalf of the first Child Abuse Prevention Act in history. Five years later, as Staff Director of the Subcommittee on Human Services of the House Select Committee on Aging, I organized some of the early hearings held on elder abuse and worked on the later amendments to the Older Americans Act that provided funding for elder abuse prevention. Then, as now, we have a troubling problem of intergenerational abuse in this nation from children to the elderly, which, has only grown worse over time. We must confront all abuse aggressively and with a commitment to reducing it as much as possible.

Our commitment to child abuse and family violence prevention has been good. I believe we have been more remiss with respect to elder abuse prevention. The opportunity to remedy is before us now. It may have been an emerging issue in the late 1970s, but it has fully arrived today. To not direct the same level of commitment to elder abuse as to other abuse constitutes a new and deeply troubling form of ageism.

Let us make elder justice more than a new term. Let's make it a new policy goal as well as a societal aspiration.

11

Dying Seniors Need Better Care

Diane E. Meier and R. Sean Morrison

Diane E. Meier is a professor of geriatrics, internal medicine, and medical ethics at the Mount Sinai School of Medicine in New York City. She is also director of the Lilian and Benjamin Hertzberg Palliative Care Institute. R. Sean Morrison is director of research at Hertzberg and an associate professor of geriatrics and internal medicine at Mount Sinai.

Medical professionals and families must accept that death is a natural and inevitable part of growing old. Most people who die in this country are elderly, and they typically die slowly of chronic diseases. While most elderly people are cared for at home by family members as they decline, the vast majority die in hospitals or nursing homes and their quality of life at the end is quite poor. Relieving suffering near the end of life should be just as important as trying to keep someone alive. Society needs to restore the balance of these two goals.

Popular images of death and dying are a jumble of gun violence, young and middle-aged adults on television fighting for life with the help of tubes, intensive care units and modern machinery, and nineteenth century images of feverish mothers or children attended at home by their grieving families and helpless physicians. In reality, these media visions bear little relationship to the actual human experience of dying in the United States. In our society, the overwhelming majority of people who die are elderly. They typically die slowly of chronic

Diane E. Meier and R. Sean Morrison, "Old Age and Care Near the End of Life," *Generations, Journal of the American Society on Aging*, vol. 28, Spring 1999. Copyright © 1999 by American Society on Aging, San Francisco, California, www.asaging.org. Reproduced by permission.

diseases, over long periods of time, with multiple coexisting problems, progressive dependency on others, and heavy care needs met mostly by family members.

Most Elderly People Die in Facilities

They spend the majority of their final months and years at home but, in most parts of the country, actually die in the hospital or nursing home surrounded by strangers. Many of these deaths become protracted and negotiated processes, with healthcare providers and family members making difficult, often wrenching, decisions about the use or discontinuation of such life-prolonging technologies as feeding tubes, ventilators, and intravenous fluids. There is abundant evidence that the quality of life during the dying process is often poor, characterized by inadequately treated physical distress, fragmented care systems, poor to absent communication between doctors and patients and families, and enormous strains on family caregiver and support systems.

Dying and Death in the United States

The median age at death in the United States is now 77 years, associated with a steady and linear decline in age-adjusted death rates since 1940. While in 1900 life expectancy at birth was less than 50 years, a girl born today may expect to live to age 79 and a boy to age 73. Those of us reaching 75 years can expect to live another ten (men) to twelve (women) years on average. This dramatic and unprecedented increase in life expectancy (equivalent to that occurring between the Stone Age and the year 1900) is due primarily to decreases in maternal and infant mortality, resulting from improved sanitation and nutrition and effective control of infectious diseases. The result of the changes in demography has been an enormous growth in the number and health of the elderly, so that by the year 2030, 20 percent of the United States' population will be over age 65, as compared to fewer than 5 percent at the turn of the century.

The Causes of Death Have Changed

While death at the turn of the century was largely attributable to infectious diseases, today the leading causes of death are heart disease, cancer, and stroke. Advances in treatment of atherosclerotic vascular disease and cancer have turned these previously rapidly fatal diseases into chronic illnesses with which people often live for many years before death. In parallel, deaths that occurred at home in the early part of the twentieth century now occur primarily in institutions (57 percent in hospitals and 17 percent in nursing homes). The reasons for its shift in location of death are complex, but they are related to Medicare reimbursement for hospital-based care, with the subsequent rise in the availability of hospitals and hospital beds and in the care burdens of chronicity and functional dependency typically accompanying life-threatening disease in the elderly. The older the patient, the higher the likelihood of death in a nursing home or hospital, with an estimated 58 percent of people over 85 spending at least some time in a nursing home in the last year of life.

> *While death at the turn of the century was largely attributable to infectious diseases, today the leading causes of death are heart disease, cancer, and stroke.*

These statistics, however, hide the fact that the majority of an older person's last months and years is still spent at home in the care of family members, with hospitalization or nursing home placement occurring only near the very end of life. Additionally, national figures such as these hide the substantial regional variation in location of death. In Portland, Oregon, for example, only 35 percent of adult deaths occur in hospitals, as compared to over 80 percent in New York City, a disparity associated at least in part with differences in regional hospital bed supply and availability of adequate community supports for the dying. Finally, national statistics also obscure the variability in the experience of dying that characterizes our highly diverse nation. For example, need for institutionalization or paid formal caregivers in the last months of life is much higher among the poor and women. Similarly, people suffering from cognitive impairment and dementia are much more likely to spend their last days in a nursing home compared to cognitively intact elderly people dying from nondementing illnesses.

Public Policies Favor Institutionalization

The incentives promoting an institutional—as opposed to home —death persist despite evidence that patients prefer to die at home and despite the existence of the Medicare hospice benefit. The hospice benefit was designed to provide substantial professional and material support (medications, equipment) to families caring for the dying at home for their last six months of life. Reasons for the low rate of utilization of the Medicare hospice benefit (serving only 11 percent of adult deaths) vary by community but include the inhibiting requirements that patients acknowledge that they are dying in order to access the services, that physicians certify a prognosis of six months or less, and that very few hours (usually four or less) of personal care home attendants are covered under the benefit. In addition, the fiscal structure of the Medicare hospice benefit lends itself well to the predictable trajectory of late-stage cancers or AIDS, but not so well to the unpredictable chronic course of other common causes of death in the elderly, like congestive heart failure, chronic lung disease, stroke, and dementing illnesses.

> *// Remarkably little is known about how death occurs in the oldest old, those over age 75. //*

Although death occurs far more commonly in the elderly than in any other age group, most research on the experience of dying has examined younger populations. Remarkably little is known about how death occurs in the oldest old, those over age 75. The largest and most detailed study of adult hospital deaths in the United States (the Study to Understand Prognoses and Preferences for Outcomes and Risks of Treatments, or SUP-PORT) focused on a relatively young population (the median age at death in the United States is 77, while the median age in SUPPORT was only 66 years) and demonstrated a high rate of untreated pain in the last few days of life, poor doctor-patient communication about the goals of medical care, and frequent use of ventilators and intensive care.

There is some evidence that costly "aggressive" and potentially burdensome life-prolonging interventions are less frequently used among the oldest patients, independent of baseline measures, which may represent a form of implicit rationing based on age. Other studies have shown consistently high levels of untreated or undertreated pain in the elderly. In one study of elderly cancer patients in nursing homes, 26 percent of patients with daily pain received no analgesic at all, and 16 percent received only Tylenol, a percentage that rose with increasing age and minority status. Another study comparing pain management in cognitively intact versus demented elderly with acute hip fracture also found a high rate of undertreatment of pain in both groups, a phenomenon that worsened with increasing age and cognitive impairment. Similarly [Charles] Cleeland's study of outpatients with cancer found that age and female sex were predictors of undertreatment, a disturbing observation given the dramatic rise in cancer prevalence with increasing age. Finally, chronic pain due to arthritis, other bone and joint disorders, and low back syndrome is probably the most common cause of distress and disability in the elderly, affecting 25–50 percent of community-dwelling older adults and, similar to cancer pain, consistently undertreated. These data suggest that the time before death among elderly people is often characterized by significant physical distress that is neither identified nor properly treated.

Dependency on Others Is Common for Elderly

Aside from pain and other sources of physical distress, the key characteristic that distinguishes the dying process as experienced by the elderly from that experienced by younger groups, is the nearly universal occurrence of long periods of functional dependency and need for family caregivers in the last months to years of life. SUPPORT, focusing on a younger age cohort, found that 55 percent of patients had persistent and serious family caregiving needs during the course of a terminal illness, a figure that rises exponentially with increasing age. Although the vast majority of caregiving (transportation, homemaker services, personal care, and more skilled nursing care) is done by unpaid family members, paid care supplements or provides the sole source of care for 15 to 20 percent of patients, especially among poor elderly women living alone. Most family caregiving is provided by women (spouses and adult daughters and daughters-in-law), placing significant strains on the physical, emotional, and socioeconomic status of the caregivers. Those ill and dependent patients without family caregivers, or those whose caregivers can no longer provide or afford needed services, are placed in nursing homes, where 20 percent of the over-age-85 population resides.

> ❝ We have transformed our view of death: Rather than an accepted part of life's experience, it is now seen as an unfamiliar and much feared event. ❞

Thus, the dying process in the oldest old is characterized by a high prevalence of untreated pain and other symptoms due to chronic conditions and is associated with progressive functional dependency, unpredictable disease course, and extensive family-caregiver needs.

Mismatch Between Current System and Needs

The current payment system is poorly matched to the needs of the chronically ill and dying elderly. Medicare fee-for-service promotes use of procedure-based payments, hospitalization, and associated specialization and discontinuity of care. Capitated managed care systems [those that receive a fixed amount of money per patient] attempt to avoid seriously ill or dying patients with high-intensity service needs, focusing instead on healthier, lower-cost patient populations. The Medicare hospice benefit was designed for patients with cancer and predictably short life spans who are willing to give up efforts to prolong life and whose families can provide for the majority of their care needs at home. None of these payment systems addresses the long-term-care needs (whether at home or in a nursing home) of chronically ill and functionally dependent individuals whose prognosis is uncertain and whose medical care usually requires simultaneous efforts to prolong life, palliate symptoms, and provide support for functional dependency.

Medicare Does Not Cover In-Home Help

Medicare does not cover costs of personal care services at home or nursing home costs for the functionally dependent elderly. Instead, these are paid for approximately equally from out-ofpocket and from Medicaid budgetary sources originally in-tended to provide care for the indigent. Even in nursing homes, standards of care focus on improvement of function and maintenance of weight and nutritional status, and evi-dence of the decline that accompanies the dying process is typ-ically regarded as a measure of substandard care. Thus, a death in a nursing home is often viewed as evidence, particularly by state regulators, of poor care rather than as an expected out-come for a frail, chronically ill older person. Similarly, quality indicators required in long-term-care settings fail to either as-sess or reward appropriate attention to such palliative measures as relief of symptoms, spiritual care, and promotion of conti-nuity, with concomitant avoidance of brink-of-death transfers to emergency rooms and hospitals.

Good News and Bad News

Again, because of unprecedented improvements in material and infant mortality and successes in the control, if not cure, of common chronic diseases, most people who die in the United States are old and frail. They die of chronic, progressive illnesses (such as end-stage heart and lung disease, cancer, stroke, and dementia) with unpredictable clinical courses and prognoses. They have unrecognized and untreated symptoms and an extremely high prevalence of functional dependency and associated family-caregiver burden. Unfortunately, current reimbursement systems are unresponsive to this patient popu-lation and their families, failing to provide primary care with continuity, support for family caregivers, and homecare ser-vices, and instead promoting fragmented specialized care tied to procedures and hospitals, for lack of any other coherent al-ternative financing mechanism.

A Call for Change

This phenomenon has prompted widespread calls for change and reorganization that would ensure accountability for out-comes, processes, and costs of care for the growing population of frail, functionally dependent, and chronically ill elderly in their last phase of life. Since care for a dying person typically includes preventive, life-prolonging, rehabilitation, and pallia-tive measures in varying proportion and intensity based upon the individual patient's needs and preferences, any new model of care will have to be responsive to this range of service requirements.

> **The time has come to restore the balance so that relief of suffering and cure of disease [are] seen as twin obligations of a medical profession that is truly dedicated to patient care.**

For example, an 88-year-old woman with congestive heart failure and deconditioning after hospitalization for pneumonia requires life-prolonging measures (treatment of heart failure, oxygen, and antibiotics), preventive measures (annual influenza vaccination), rehabilitation (home physical therapy to restore independent bed-to-chair mobility), and palliative care (advance care planning, appointment of a healthcare proxy, treatment of depression, diuretics, oxygen, and low-dose opiates for breathing difficulties). Since her daughter works during the day, she also needs a 12-hour-a-day home health aide because she is unable to care for herself independently. Thus, the model of care needed provides simultaneous life-prolonging, palliative, and personal care (for this patient they are nearly one and the same), and, given the difficulty of prognosticating time of death in cases of heart failure, will have to continue to do so for the remainder of the patient's life. . . .

Care Must Reflect Needs of Patients

Substantial change using approaches such as these will be necessary if the healthcare system is to bear any relationship to the needs of the patients seeking care—patients who are predominantly old and chronically ill and in urgent need of help truly fitted to their needs. Though the problem is daunting, the increase in attention to medical education, research, and clinical service delivery for patients near the end of life is an indication that the need to begin the process of change has been recognized. The next steps, testing new models and seeing what works, will define the new structure of healthcare services for future generations.

Whereas a century ago, virtually everyone died at home, surrounded by family and cared for by physicians whose primary role was the relief of suffering, today the vast majority of Americans die within institutions, surrounded by medical technology and physicians who believe there is nothing else that they can do.

Society's View of Death Has Been Transformed

While the past one hundred years have seen tremendous advances in the treatment of disease such that previously fatal illnesses like diabetes and congestive heart failure have become chronic conditions, this progress has come at a substantial cost. We have transformed our view of death: Rather than an accepted part of life's experience, it is now seen as an unfamiliar and much feared event. The majority of Americans have never witnessed a loved one die (a common experience at the turn of the century), and physicians are ill-trained and ill-equipped to care for dying patients, and uncomfortable taking responsibility for this care. It is clear that the time has come to restore the balance so that relief of suffering and cure of disease [are] seen as twin obligations of a medical profession that is truly dedicated to patient care.

12

The System of Elderly Care Needs to Accommodate Gay and Lesbian Seniors

Tamara Thompson

Tamara Thompson holds a master's of social welfare in gerontology from the University of California–Berkeley. She has published several articles on gay and lesbian aging issues.

The gay and lesbian baby boomers who came of age during the gay rights movement of the 1960s are the first truly "out" generation. As boomers age, the country will need to care for an unprecedentedly large group of homosexual seniors. Although the need for senior housing, assisted living help, and skilled nursing care will be great, most programs that currently serve the elderly are not sensitive to the needs of lesbian, gay, bisexual, and transgendered (LGBT) people. Changes are needed throughout the elder-care system in order to ensure that gay and lesbian seniors are treated with respect.

For decades, lesbian and gay seniors have been virtually invisible, both within the gay community and society at large. But as the vanguard of the gay rights movement ages and looks to retirement, attention is swiftly turning toward issues affecting the old. Adding to the urgency, the number of LGBT [lesbian, gay, bisexual, and transgendered] seniors—already more than 3 million nationwide—is expected to more than double by

2030 as the baby boom generation ages. Most of them will need senior housing, assisted living help, and skilled nursing care.

"It's time for the community to start paying attention to what it's going to offer for old lesbians and gays," says Nancy Nystrom, a Michigan-based researcher and community organizer who studies and works with old lesbians. "The critical needs that are emerging for old LGBT people are housing that is affordable, medical care that is non-discriminatory and safe, and social support structures that include the old within all facets of LGBT life."

Queer Seniors Face Ageism in Gay Community

Queer elders also face the additional challenge of confronting agephobia within a very youth-oriented gay community. "Older lesbians and gays experience a double whammy—they're marginalized in the LGBT community for being old, and in the senior community for being gay," says Terry Kaelber, executive director of Senior Action in a Gay Environment (SAGE), the nation's oldest and largest social services organization for lesbian and gay seniors.

> *The right of queer seniors to comfortably be themselves without fear of discrimination or reprisal must be protected.*

SAGE has chapters throughout the United States and Canada and sponsors an annual National Conference on Aging in the LGBT Communities to highlight LGBT aging issues. Lesbian and gay aging is finally showing up on the radar of mainstream organizations, too. The American Society on Aging has created a Lesbian and Gay Aging Issues Network and now offers an extensive track of workshops devoted to LGBT issues during its annual conference each year. Workshops range from elder sexuality, to late-life legal planning, to long-term care for LGBT people, to mental health issues associated with aging.

All signs say that the need is great.

A recent study done by SAGE in conjunction with the Brookdale Center on Aging at Hunter College in Manhattan found that gay and lesbian seniors are "twice as likely [66 percent vs. 33 percent] as the general population of seniors to live alone." The reason is no big mystery: More than 75 percent of LGBT people never have children, and others are estranged from their extended families because of their lifestyles. But living alone doesn't just mean isolation and loneliness—it can mean far worse.

Isolation Leads to Higher Dementia Risk

In 2001, scientists at the Stockholm Gerontology Research Center at Karolinska Institute in Sweden found that the more socially isolated seniors are, the more likely they are to develop dementia. The study—comprised of 1,200 men and women who were over age 75—showed that those who live alone, have no friends or have bad relationships with their children are up to 60 percent more likely to develop dementia than those who have more socially satisfying encounters.

That statistic has staggering implications, but it's also just the tip of the iceberg. Living alone is just one of the challenges that aging gays and lesbians face because of who they are. For example:

- Queer seniors who enter mainstream care facilities often face discrimination and abuse if they remain open about their sexual identities. Few caregivers have been trained to recognize and be sensitive to the needs of gay and lesbian elders, and homophobic peers can quickly create a hostile environment for an LGBT person who is out.
- Traditional facilities that serve the elderly don't generally make provisions for gay and lesbian seniors. Physical contact between same-sex individuals is routinely discouraged in care-home settings, and couples are often separated. By contrast, many mainstream facilities allow straight, married couples to share private rooms.
- LGBT people face additional emotional challenges in coping with death of a partner because caregivers and families may not recognize or acknowledge the significance of their loss—or their right to inherit shared property.
- In many states, hospitalized gays and lesbians are still routinely denied visits from their longtime partners, adding even more stress to a health crisis.

There are many horror stories, but there is progress, too. SAGE in particular has made great strides in outreach to LGBT seniors and their caregivers. Besides sensitivity training for

National Association of Area Agencies on Aging, "Home and Community-Based Services," www.n4a.org. Copyright © by the National Association of Area Agencies on Aging. Reproduced by permission.

David Crary, "Bias Against the Elderly: As Boomers Become Seniors, Ageism Becomes Hot Topic," Associated Press, August 30, 2004. Copyright © 2004 by the Associated Press. All rights reserved. Reproduced by permission.

Tamara Thompson, "The Eldercare System Must Welcome Gay and Lesbian Seniors," 2004. Copyright © 2004 by Tamara Thompson. Reproduced by permission.

health care professionals, SAGE offers friendly visitor programs for homebound seniors, social clubs, a drop-in center, social worker visits and scores of other activities and initiatives. SAGE is an advocate for queer seniors everywhere, but most of its work is centered in New York City.

Although awareness is slowly growing nationwide, queer seniors in most parts of the country remain mostly overlooked and underserved. It's high time that changed. Social workers, medical professionals, nursing home employees, at-home aides and others who work with seniors should receive training so that they can understand LGBT seniors and their needs. The formal policies of nursing homes, board and care facilities and hospitals should be updated to embrace sexual diversity so that they no longer discriminate—whether intentionally or not—on the basis of orientation. Above all, the right of queer seniors to comfortably be themselves without fear of discrimination or reprisal must be protected.

Glossary

activities of daily living (ADLs): Activities necessary for individuals to take care of themselves independently. ADLs include bathing, eating, dressing, grooming, going to the toilet, taking medication, and transferring from a bed to chair.

aging in place: Growing old in one's own home rather than in a nursing home or other facility for the elderly.

assisted-living facility: Housing for older people who cannot live on their own but do not need as much care as a nursing home provides. People who live in assisted-living facilities usually have their own private apartments and receive help with such things as medication management, bathing, and housekeeping. Assisted-living facilities are typically very expensive, and government programs such as Medicaid and Medicare do not help pay for them.

baby boomers: The 76 million Americans born between 1946 and 1964, following World War II. "Boomers" are the country's largest demographic group, and their aging will have profound consequences for the country in terms of social services, housing, and health care expenditures. The last of the baby boomers will reach age fifty-five in 2019, and it is estimated that 20 percent of the U.S. population will be over sixty-five by 2030.

elder abuse: Any physical, psychological, financial, or sexual mistreatment of an older adult. Also includes neglect, which is the withholding of care or necessities from an individual, and self-neglect, the inability of an elderly person to take care of themselves.

hospice: A philosophy of caring for terminally ill people that is characterized by concern for relieving symptoms and pain, increasing general well-being, and providing spiritual comfort for those who are dying.

institutionalization: A term used to describe the long-term placement of individuals in medical settings or mental facilities. When the term is applied to the elderly, it typically refers to their being cared for in nursing homes or hospitals.

instrumental activities of daily living (IADLs): Activities that are not necessary for basic self-care, but which are still very important to everyday life. IADLs include the ability to use a telephone, prepare meals, shop for food and clothing, do housework, use transportation, and handle financial matters.

long-term care (LTC): A wide range of supports and services provided to individuals who are unable to live independently because of chronic

98

illness or disability. Although LTC may be provided in a person's home, most LTC facilities are nursing homes.

Medicaid: A government health insurance program for low-income people. It is funded jointly by federal and state money and is administered by the states, each of which has its own Medicaid program. In California, Medicaid is known as MediCal. To qualify for Medicaid, individuals must pass a means test to prove that they are poor. The biggest expense of Medicaid is nursing home care for elderly people. In 2002 Medicaid paid for 47 percent of the total long-term care costs nationwide.

Medicare: The federal government's health insurance program for the elderly and disabled. Established in 1965 as a set of amendments to Social Security, Medicare is available to anyone sixty-five or older, younger people with disabilities, and people with permanent kidney failure. The program has two parts: Part A (hospital insurance) and Part B (Medicare insurance, which helps cover doctors' services, outpatient care, and some other services that Part A does not cover). A recently added prescription drug benefit will take effect in 2006. Medicare does not pay for nursing home stays longer than thirty days, a major issue of financial concern for the elderly. In 2003 Medicare provided health coverage for 40 million Americans. Enrollment is expected to reach 77 million by 2031, when the baby boom generation is fully enrolled. Medicare is administered by the Centers for Medicare and Medicaid Services (CMS) in the U.S. Department of Health and Human Services.

medigap insurance: Private insurance policies that cover the difference between what Medicare pays for and what is actually charged for medical services.

nursing home: Any residential facility that provides some degree of medical care to residents. There are three levels of care: skilled, intermediate, and extended. A skilled nursing facility offers a full range of medical treatment and personal care to residents. An intermediate care facility offers health-related care for patients who need a lower level of assistance. An extended care facility is primarily a transitional or rehabilitation facility that offers short-term convalescence after a hospital stay.

Older Americans Act (OAA): A 1965 federal law that authorized and established funding for a wide variety of direct services for older adults, such as senior centers, nutrition programs, case management, and information and referral programs.

Olmstead **decision:** A landmark 1999 Supreme Court ruling that interpreted the Americans with Disabilities Act (ADA) to mean that elderly and disabled individuals should be allowed to live in the least restrictive setting possible. The *Olmstead* decision has caused a shift away from the institutionalization of the elderly and toward more home-based care.

palliative care: Any type of medical care that focuses on reducing the severity of pain and slowing the progress of disease rather than trying to cure it. The goal of palliative care—sometimes called "comfort care"—is to improve the quality of life rather than prolong it.

pay-go system: Short for "pay-as-you-go," an approach to paying for Social Security in which today's workers contribute money that is used to pay for benefits for individuals who are currently retired. Under the pay-go system, current workers pay for current benefits, rather than the money being set aside to pay for their own future benefits.

skilled nursing facility (SNF): A residential care facility for people who require constant medical attention but at a lower level of care than in a hospital. Usually the residents are elderly, but younger people who need skilled medical care often reside there as well. About 80 percent of skilled nursing facilities in the United States are run by for-profit companies.

Social Security: The federal government program that pays retirement benefits to the elderly and death benefits to surviving family members. Social Security was created in 1935 as part of President Franklin Delano Roosevelt's New Deal. The program is funded by a payroll tax that is half paid by employers and half by workers. Retirement benefits are paid monthly according to a formula based on how much a person earned over their lifetime. Social Security operates under a pay-go system; current year benefits are paid from current taxes. Because of the large number of baby boomers that will soon retire, taxes are not expected to cover expenses by 2015. There is a great deal of debate about what should be done. One of the most likely scenarios is the partial privatization of Social Security through the creation of individual accounts. Current proposals call for individuals to be allowed to use these accounts to put some of their Social Security money into the stock market. There is much controversy surrounding this plan. Other ideas include reducing benefit payments or again raising the age at which people can collect Social Security.

supplemental security income (SSI): A federal program administered by Social Security that provides a monthly payment to low-income disabled individuals who cannot work and who have no other income. To qualify for SSI, individuals must pass a means test to prove that they are poor. Many elderly people receive SSI, which is meant to help pay for basic necessities such as food, shelter, and clothing. In most states, being eligible for SSI means an individual is also entitled to medical coverage through Medicaid.

Organizations to Contact

The editors have compiled the following list of organizations concerned with the issues presented in this book. The descriptions are derived from materials provided by the organizations. All have publications or information available for interested readers. The list was compiled on the date of publication of the present volume; the information provided here may change. Be aware that many organizations take several weeks or longer to respond to inquiries, so allow as much time as possible.

AARP
601 E St. NW, Washington, DC 20049
(800) 424-3410
e-mail: member@aarp.org • Web site: www.aarp.org

AARP, formerly known as the American Association of Retired Persons, is a nonpartisan association that seeks to improve the aging experience for all Americans. It is committed to the preservation of Social Security and Medicare. AARP publishes the magazine *Modern Maturity* and the newsletter *AARP Bulletin*. Issue statements and congressional testimony can be found at the Web site.

Administration on Aging (AOA)
330 Independence Ave. SW, Washington, DC 20201
(202) 619-0724 • fax: (202) 357-3555
e-mail: aoainfo@aoa.gov • Web site: www.aoa.dhhs.gov

The AOA works with a number of organizations, senior centers, and local service providers to help older people remain independent. It also works to protect the rights of the elderly, prevent crime and violence against older persons, and investigate health care fraud. AOA's publications include fact sheets on issues such as age discrimination, elder abuse, and Alzheimer's disease. Additional publications are available through AOA's National Aging Information Center.

Alzheimer's Association
919 North Michigan Ave., Suite 1100, Chicago, IL 60611-1676
(800) 272-3900 • fax: (312) 335-1110
e-mail: info@alz.org • Web site: www.alz.org

The Alzheimer's Association is committed to finding a cure for Alzheimer's and helping those affected by the disease. The association funds research into the causes and treatments of Alzheimer's disease and provides education and support for people diagnosed with the condition, their families, and caregivers. Position statements and fact sheets are available at its Web site.

American Geriatrics Society (AGS)
350 Fifth Ave., Suite 801, New York, NY 10118
(212) 308-1414 • fax: (212) 832-8646
e-mail: info@americangeriatrics.org
Web site: www.americangeriatrics.org

The AGS is a professional organization of health care providers that aims to improve the health and well-being of all older adults. AGS helps shape attitudes, policies, and practices regarding health care for older people. The society's publications include the book *The American Geriatrics Society's Complete Guide to Aging and Health*, the magazines *Journal of the American Geriatrics Society* and *Annals of Long-Term Care: Clinical Care and Aging*, and *The AGS Newsletter*.

American Society on Aging
833 Market St., Suite 511, San Francisco, CA 94103-1824
(415) 974-9600 • fax: (415) 974-0300
e-mail: info@asaging.org • Web site: www.asaging.org

The American Society on Aging is an organization of health care and social service professionals, researchers, educators, businesspersons, senior citizens, and policy makers that is concerned with all aspects of aging and works to enhance the well-being of older individuals. Its publications include the bimonthly newspaper *Aging Today* and the quarterly journal *Generations*.

Family Caregiver Alliance (FCA)
80 Montgomery St., Suite 1100, San Francisco, CA 94104
(800) 445-8106 • fax: (415) 434-3508
e-mail: info@caregiver.org • Web site: www.caregiver.org

Founded in 1977, FCA is a community-based nonprofit organization that serves the needs of families and friends providing long-term care at home. FCA offers programs at the national, state, and local levels to support and assist caregivers and is a public voice for caregivers through education, services, research, and advocacy. Its Web site offers a wide range of information on caregiver issues and resources, including numerous fact sheets, policy papers, and other publications.

Medicare Rights Center (MRC)
1460 Broadway, 17th Fl., New York, NY 10036
(212) 869-3850 • fax: (212) 869-3532
e-mail: info@medicarerights.org • Web site: www.medicarerights.org

The MRC is a national organization that helps ensure that older adults receive affordable quality health care. It publishes a wide variety of Medicare materials, including a series of self-help pamphlets on Medicare issues and numerous booklets on Medicare-related topics.

National Association for Home Care (NAHC)
228 Seventh St. SE, Washington, DC 20003
(202) 547-7424 • fax: (202) 547-3540
e-mail: pr@nahc.org • Web site: www.nahc.org

The NAHC believes that Americans should receive health care and social services in their own homes. It represents home care agencies, hospices, and home care aide organizations. NAHC publishes the quarterly newspaper *Homecare News* and the monthly magazine *Caring*.

National Association of Area Agencies on Aging (N4A)
1730 Rhode Island Ave. NW, Suite 1200, Washington, DC 20036
(202) 872-0888 • fax: (202) 872-0057
Web site: www.n4a.org

The N4A on Aging is the umbrella organization for the 655 area agencies on aging in the United States. Its mission is to help older people and those with disabilities live with dignity and choices in their homes and communities for as long as possible. The N4A Web site provides links to Area Agencies on Aging in all states as well as to other government organizations that serve seniors. It also acts as a portal for the Eldercare Locator, a national toll-free number to assist older people and their families in finding community services for seniors anywhere in the country.

National Center on Elder Abuse (NCEA)
1201 Fifteenth St. NW, Suite 350, Washington, DC 20005
(202) 898-2586 • fax: (202) 898-2583
e-mail: ncea@nasua.org • Web site: www.elderabusecenter.org

The NCEA is a gateway to resources on elder abuse, neglect, and exploitation. The NCEA is funded by the U.S. Administration on Aging. The center offers news and resources; collaborates on research; provides consultation, education, and training; identifies and provides information about promising practices and interventions; answers inquiries and requests for information; operates a Listserv forum for professionals; and advises on program and policy development.

National Citizens' Coalition for Nursing Home Reform
1424 Sixteenth St. NW, Suite 202, Washington, DC 20036-2211
(202) 332-2275 • fax: (202) 332-2949
e-mail: nccnhr@nccnhr.org • Web site: www.nccnhr.org

The National Citizens' Coalition for Nursing Home Reform provides information and leadership on federal and state regulatory and legislative policy development and strategies to improve nursing home care and life for residents. Publications include the book *Nursing Homes: Getting Good Care There*, NCCNHR's newsletter *Quality Care Advocate*, and fact sheets on issues such as abuse and neglect, restraints use, and how to choose a nursing home.

National Committee to Preserve Social Security and Medicare
10 G St. NE, Suite 600, Washington, DC 20004
(800) 966-1935 • fax: (202) 216-0451
e-mail: general@ncpssm.org • Web site: www.ncpssm.org

The National Committee to Preserve Social Security and Medicare is a nonprofit, nonpartisan membership organization. Through advocacy, education, services, and grassroots efforts, the committee works to ensure a secure retirement for all Americans. Its Web site is a good place to find information and analyses regarding Social Security, Medicare, and other retirement issues.

National Council on the Aging (NCOA)
300 D St. SW, Suite 801, Washington, DC 20024
(202) 479-1200 • fax: (202) 479-0735
e-mail: info@ncoa.org • Web site: www.ncoa.org

The NCOA is an association of organizations and professionals dedicated to promoting the dignity, self-determination, well-being, and contributions of older people. It advocates business practices, societal attitudes, and public policies that promote vital aging. NCOA's quarterly magazine, *Journal of the National Council on the Aging*, provides tools and insights for community service organizations.

National Hospice and Palliative Care Organization (NHPCO)
1700 Diagonal Rd., Suite 625, Alexandria, VA 22314
(703) 837-1500 • fax: (703) 837-1233
e-mail: nhpco_info@nhpco.org • Web site: www.nhpco.org

The NHPCO (originally the National Hospice Organization) was founded in 1978 to educate the public about the benefits of hospice care for the terminally ill and their families. It seeks to promote the idea that with the proper care and pain medication, the terminally ill can live out their lives comfortably and in the company of their families. The organization opposes euthanasia and assisted suicide. It conducts educational and training programs for administrators and caregivers in numerous aspects of hospice care. The NHPCO publishes grief and bereavement guides, brochures such as *Hospice Care: A Consumer's Guide to Selecting a Hospice Program* and *Communicating Your End-of-Life Wishes*, and the book *Hospice Care: A Celebration*.

Senior Action in a Gay Environment (SAGE)
305 Seventh Ave., 16th Fl., New York, NY 10001
(212) 741-2247 • fax: (212) 366-1947
e-mail: sageusa@aol.com • Web site: www.sageusa.org

SAGE is the world's largest and oldest organization devoted specifically to meeting the needs of aging LGBT (lesbian, gay, bisexual, and transgendered) people. SAGE provides direct services to LGBT seniors in New York City and works to increase awareness of gay aging through education and advocacy throughout the United States.

Bibliography

Books

Henry Aaron, John Shoven, and Benjamin Friedman, eds.	*Should the United States Privatize Social Security?* Boston: MIT Press, 1999.
Stuart Altman and David Shactman	*Policies for an Aging Society.* Baltimore: Johns Hopkins University Press, 2002.
Sue Blevins	*Medicare's Midlife Crisis.* Washington, DC: Cato Institute, 2001.
Ira Byock	*Dying Well: Peace and Possibilities at the End of Life.* New York: Riverhead, 1998.
Ken Dychtwald	*Age Power: How the Twenty-First Century Will Be Ruled by the New Old.* New York: Penguin Putnam, 1999.
Lita Epstein	*The Complete Idiot's Guide to Social Security.* Indianapolis: Alpha, 2002.
Peter Ferrara and Michael Tanner	*Common Cents, Common Dreams—a Layman's Guide to Social Security Privatization.* Washington, DC: Cato Institute, 1998.
Donald Gelfand	*The Aging Network: Programs and Services.* 5th ed. New York: Springer, 1999.
Neil Gilbert	*Transformation of the Welfare State: The Silent Surrender of Public Responsibility.* New York: Oxford University Press, 2002.
Margaret Morganroth Gullette	*Aged by Culture.* Chicago: University of Chicago Press, 2004.
Mary Hird	*Elder Abuse, Neglect, and Maltreatment: What Can Be Done to Stop It.* Pittsburgh: Dorrance, 2003.
Harry Moody	*Aging: Concepts and Controversies.* 3rd ed. Thousand Oaks, CA: Pine Forge, 2000.
Patricia Smith et al.	*Alzheimer's for Dummies.* Hoboken, NJ: Wiley, 2003.
U.S. Department of Transportation	*Transportation for a Maturing Society.* Washington, DC: U.S. Department of Transportation, 1997.

Periodicals

Edmund Andrews	"Economic View: Social Security Reform, with One Big Catch," *New York Times*, December 12, 2004.

106

Associated Press   "Democrats Say Medicare Law Could Eat into Social Security Benefits," *Boston Herald*, July 21, 2004.

Robert M. Ball   "How to Fix Social Security? It Doesn't Have to Be Hard," *Aging Today*, March/April 2004.

Wendy Bonafazi   "Who Pays for Long Term Care?" *Contemporary Long Term Care*, October 1998.

James J. Callahan Jr.   "Giving the Elderly Options on Independent Living," *Boston Globe*, November 24, 2002.

Consumer Reports   "How Will You Pay for Your Old Age?" October 1997.

Stephen Crystal   "Elder Abuse: The Latest Crisis," *Public Interest*, 1987.

Robert B. Friedland   "Caregivers and Long-Term Care Needs in the 21st Century: Will Public Policy Meet the Challenge?" Issue brief, Long-Term Care Financing Project, Georgetown University, Washington, DC, 2004.

Victor Fuchs   "Health Care for the Elderly: How Much? Who Will Pay for It?" *Health Affairs*, January/February 1999.

William Gale   "Retirement Saving and Long-Term Care Needs: An Overview," Retirement Security Project, Brookings Institution and Tax Policy Center, 2004.

Vicki Haddock   "Seniors Can't Go Home Again—Medi-Cal Rules Force State's Elderly into Costly Nursing Facilities," *San Francisco Chronicle*, August 1, 2004.

Health Policy Institute   "Medicaid and an Aging Population," Fact sheet, Long-Term Care Financing Project, Georgetown University, Washington, DC, 2004.

Marsha King   "Concerns of Elder Gays—Aging Poses New Healthcare, Legal Challenges for Partners," *Seattle Times*, October 7, 2001.

N.R. Kleinfield   "Lillian and Julia—a Twilight of Fear: Bowed by Age and Battered by an Addicted Nephew," *New York Times*, December 12, 2004.

Paul Krugman   "Inventing a Crisis," *New York Times*, December 7, 2004.

Michael Lemonick and Alice Park-Mankato   "The Nun Study—How One Scientist and 678 Sisters Are Helping Unlock the Secrets of Alzheimer's," *Time*, May 14, 2001.

Phillip Longman   "Fixing Social Security," *Fortune*, November 1, 2004.

New York Times   "How Not to Save Social Security," September 23, 2004.

Julie Phillips   "Baby Boomers Come of Age and Generation X
                                Sounds Off," *Utne Reader*, March/April 1994.

Barbara Stucki and   "Can Aging Boomers Avoid Nursing Homes?"
Janemarie Mulvey   *Consumers' Research Magazine*, August 2000.

Shankar Vedantam   "Reagans' Experience Alters Outlook for
                                Alzheimer's Patients," *Washington Post*, June 14,
                                2004.

Index

108